RELIGIOUS WORLDS

A Dragon's World Ltd Imprint

Dragon's World Ltd
Limpsfield
Surrey RH8 0DY
Great Britain

First published in Australia 1985
by
Hill of Content Publishing Company Pty Ltd
86 Bourke Street, Melbourne, Victoria
Copyright © Text Max Charlesworth, 1985
            Illustrations Robert Ingpen, 1985
Typeset by Abb-Typesetting Pty Ltd, Melbourne
Printed in Hong Kong by Everbest Printing Co. Ltd.

Cataloguing-in-publication data

Charlesworth, Max, 1925- .
  Religious worlds.

  ISBN 1 85028 039 8

  1. Religions — Juvenile literature. I. Ingpen, Robert,
  1936- . II. Title.

RELIGIOUS WORLDS

MAX CHARLESWORTH AND ROBERT INGPEN

Contents

RELIGIONS   5

THE RELIGION OF THE JEWS — God and the Chosen People   17

THE CHRISTIAN WORLD   22

MUHAMMAD AND ISLAM   30

HINDUISM — Gods, Yogas, and Gurus   36

THE BUDDHA'S WAY OF ENLIGHTENMENT   42

CONFUCIUS AND THE CHINESE WAY   48

AUSTRALIAN ABORIGINAL RELIGION — The Sacred Land   52

RELIGIONS OF THE NORTH AMERICAN INDIANS   58

REFLECTIONS   63

Religions

How many religions do you know of? Perhaps you know of the Christian religion, the Jewish religion, the Hindu religion, and the Islamic religion. Well, that's a beginning, but we've mentioned only four religions, and there are many, many more religions than four.

There are hundreds and hundreds of religions.

Some religions are big religions, like Christianity and Hinduism which have millions and millions of members. Some religions are small religions, like the religion of the Aboriginal Aranda people in Central Australia which has only a few hundred members.

Some religions are old, like Hinduism which began about 3000 years ago. Some religions are new, like Mormonism, which began 150 years ago.

Some religions have died, like the religion of the ancient Greeks, with their gods, Zeus, Athene, Plutus, Aphrodite and so on. Some religions have just been born, like the Unification Church of the Reverend Moon (the 'Moonies').

Some religions have spread all over the world, like Christianity and Islam. Some religions have remained in the one place, like the religions of the various tribes in Africa or in New Guinea or Australia.

Ever since human beings began they seem to have had religions, just as they seem to have been interested in art — drawing and painting and dancing and making music.

Each religion is like a little world all of its own — a world in which people who believe in that religion live out their lives. And there are hundreds and hundreds of these religious worlds.

What are religions about?

Have you ever wondered about these questions?

Why is there anything at all? There might have been nothing — no thing — at all, so why do things exist instead of there being nothing?

Where has everything come from? Did someone make the world and begin it all? Or did it just happen, just like that, out of nowhere and out of nothing?

What is the purpose of everything? Do things just come and go and live and die without any reason? Or is there a reason?

Is this a good world, or a bad world, or a world that is neither good nor bad?

Are human beings like us especially important? Or are we no more important than stones, or trees, or animals? Are we more valuable than cabbages, mosquitos, moths, fishes, cats?

RELIGIONS

MIDDLE EAST
- Egyptian
- Manicheeism
- Parsee
- Zoroastrianism
- Judaism
  - Orthodox
  - Hasidism
  - Reform

CHRISTIAN
- Catholic
  - Eastern
  - Latin
- Orthodox
  - Greek
  - Roumanian
  - Russian
- Church of England
  - Episcopalian
  - Methodist
- Reformed Churches
  - Lutheranism
  - Calvinism
  - Baptist
  - Congregational

ISLAM
- Sunni
- Shi'te
- Sufi

INDIAN
- Sikhism
- Jainism
- Buddhism
  - Tantrism
  - Mahayana
  - Theravada
- Vedism
- Hinduism

CHINESE
- Confucianism
- Taoism
- Buddhism

JAPANESE
- Buddhism
  - Pure Land
  - Nichiren
  - Zen
- Animism
- Shintoism

SOUTH AMERICA
- Mexican
  - Olmec
  - Toltec
  - Aztec
- Mayan
- Peruvian
  - Chavin
  - Paracas
  - Nazca
  - Mochica
  - Inca

TRIBAL
- North American
  - Cree
  - Sioux
  - Algonkin
- New Guinean
  - Tolki
  - Motu
  - Chimbu
- African
  - Dinka
  - Nuer
  - Yoruba
- Asian
  - Animism
- Australian
  - Murngin
  - Walbiri
  - Aranda

Do our lives have any meaning? Or do we just live and die, here today and gone tomorrow, like plants and animals, without any special reason?

How should I live? Why should I be good? Why shouldn't I do whatever I would just like to do?

When I die, is that the end of me? Or will I keep on living in some way after my body dies?

Why do people suffer from illness and disease? Why do people do bad things and hurt themselves and other people? Why are there cyclones and earthquakes and bushfires and floods?

Is this world I live in the only world there is? Or is there another quite different world beyond this world? Are there beings in that other world — spirits, gods, angels — that are quite different from the beings in this world?

These are BIG questions and DEEP questions.

They are BIG questions because they are about everything. Did everything have a beginning? Does everything have a meaning? And so on.

And they are DEEP questions because they go right down to the basis of things. Is there a reason for things existing? Why should I be good? Why is there evil in the world? And so on.

Religions try to give answers to these BIG and DEEP questions. So Christianity and Judaism and Buddhism and all the other religions try to explain why things exist, whether our lives have a meaning, how we should

live, how we can cope with death and suffering and evil, whether there is another world beyond this one, and so on.

That's what religions are: they are attempts to answer the BIG and DEEP questions about the world and about our lives. That's why people become religious: they want to find answers to those questions.

Kinds of religions

The various religions are different ways of answering the BIG and DEEP questions. They provide different maps to help people to find out where they are and which direction they should travel.

Some religions say that there is one God; others say that there are many Gods; and still others say there are no Gods at all.

Some religions say that God is in the world and in us human beings; others say that God is over and beyond the world and that God exists in a very different way from the things in the world and from human beings. (For example, they say that, unlike us, God has not been born and that 'he' will never die; and that, unlike us, 'he' is completely good and knows absolutely everything and can do anything 'he' wants to.)

Some religions say that this world and this life are not very important but that the other world that is beyond this world is much more important: others say that our life in this world is very important and that God has come into this world.

Some religions have sacred books and say that they contain messages from God

to us. Others don't have any sacred books.

Some religions have special people called priests and priestesses who explain God's message to ordinary people: others do not have special people like these and say that ordinary people can get in touch with God for themselves.

Some religions are very organised, with churches and strict rules about how things should be done: others are not organised at all.

Some religions have lots of special prayers and ceremonies: others say that you can get in touch with God without prayers and ceremonies.

Are religions fairy stories?

Some people say that religions are just fairy stories. They say that just as children tell themselves fairy stories and imagine that they are true, so religious people think that their imaginary stories about Gods are true. But the religious stories are not true: they are simply childish make-believe. Grown-up people, they say, do not need to believe in such stories. We can explain everything about the world and about human beings without believing in these religious stories.

However, religious people — Christians and Jews and Hindus and Buddhists — say that religions are not childish fairy stories at all. They say that their religions are ways of answering the BIG and DEEP questions.

Religious people would say to people who think that religions are just fairy stories: 'Well then, how would you try to answer the BIG and DEEP questions: what have you got to say about the beginnings of everything, and the

importance of human life, and why we should be good, and whether death is the end of everything, and why there is evil and suffering in the world: can you provide us with a map to help us to find out where we are and what direction we should travel: can you really explain everything about the world and about human beings without some kind of religious belief ?'

In this book we are going to look at some of the different kinds of religions, and try to find out what the people who live in each religious world believe and think about. These are the religions we are going to talk about: **Judaism, Christianity, Islam, Hinduism, Buddhism, Confucianism, Australian Aboriginal Religion** and **American Indian Religion**.

We will also say something about those people who claim that religions are fairy tales (such people are called *atheists*), and those who claim that we cannot ever know the answers to the BIG and DEEP questions (such people are called *agnostics*). The Greek word for 'God' is *theos*, so a person who doesn't believe in God is called an *a-theist*. People who believe there is only one God are called *mono-theists* — from the Greek words *monos* (one) and *theos* (God). Those who believe there are many Gods are called *poly-theists* — from the Greek words *poly* (many) and *theos* (God). The Greek word for a person who knows is *gnostic*, so one who does not know is called an *a-gnostic*.

We will have to ask ourselves whether one religion is better than or truer than another. For example, is Christianity (or Judaism or Buddhism) the only really true religion, and are all the others wrong? Or are the different religions simply different ways of expressing the same basic ideas?

TRIBAL   ISLAM   JUDAISM   CHRISTIANITY   HINDUISM   BUDDHISM   CONFUCIANISM

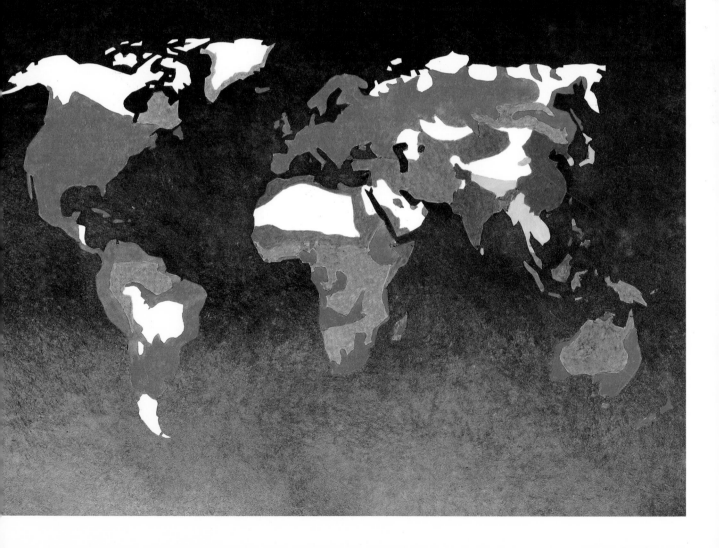

Religious Worlds

The Religion of the Jews

GOD AND THE CHOSEN PEOPLE

About 4000 years ago the Jewish (or Hebrew) people came together as a nation. In the old Jewish stories the leaders of this new nation were called Abraham and Isaac and Jacob.

Later the Jewish people were conquered by the Egyptians and they were forced to go to Egypt and work as slaves. After a long time they were saved by a leader called Moses who led them out of Egypt to the land that is now called Israel. This happened about 1250 years before the time of Jesus Christ.

Moses said that God had spoken to him and given him a message for the Jewish people. God told Moses that the Jews were his 'chosen people' and that he was going to set up an agreement (or 'covenant') with them.

'I will agree to care especially for them', said God,

'if they will love me and obey my Law'.

'I will be the God of the Jewish people if they will be my people', said God.

GOD'S LAW God also gave Moses a Law for the Jewish people. God's Law contains a number of rules or commandments, such as:

- You must love God, who is your Lord, in a very special way.
- You must love and respect your mother and father.
- You must not kill other people.
- You must not have sexual relationships with another man or woman unless you are married to that person.
- You must not steal.
- You must spend one day each week thinking about God and praying to him.

God's Law also contains rules about what to eat and drink such as:

- You must not eat meat with blood in it.
- You must not eat pork.
- You must not drink milk after eating meat.

These rules remind Jews that everything they do has something to do with God.

THE TORAH Later on, all the things that God said to Moses were written down and became the first part of the book called the Old Testament. The other parts of the book tell the story of the Jewish people.

All the teachings and commandments and rules revealed by God to the Jewish people are called the *Torah* (the Hebrew word for 'teaching' or 'instruction'). Jewish people believe that the *Torah* is especially sacred because it is the word of God himself.

18

In the *Torah*

- God says that he is the only God. There is only one God and those who believe there are many Gods are wrong.
- God also says that he has created everything, and everything (including us) is completely dependent on him. We owe everything we have to God.
- Gods says that we human beings are created in his 'image' and that we are the most important things in the world — much more important than animals and other things. We must not, however, become too proud and think that we are just as good as God and that we can do without God.
- God says that if we love him and obey his commandments we will be able to live with him in the next life, after we die.

Jewish people also believe that at some future time a special messenger who is called the *Messiah* will come from God. He will make all quarrels and wars stop and people will then live peacefully together. This will be 'the Kingdom of God', when God will rule over the whole world.

In the Jewish religion there are no priests or churches. Instead of priests the Jews have rabbis who are religious teachers: instead of churches they have synagogues which are meeting places for saying prayers, reading the *Torah*, and special ceremonies.

Most Jewish children learn about their religion from their mothers and fathers and many religious ceremonies are held at home. For example, the Passover or Pesach ceremony is held to remind Jewish people of the time when they escaped from slavery in Egypt thousands of years ago. In this ceremony the children and their parents eat flat unleavened bread to remind themselves that the ancient Jews had to leave Egypt so quickly that the dough for the bread did not have time to rise. They also eat cooked lamb to remind themselves of the lamb's blood put on the Hebrews' doors in Egypt. (God sent his angel to each of the Egyptian houses to punish them and the blood showed the angel which houses to leave alone.)

And they eat bitter herbs to remind them of the hard and bitter time they had in Egypt.

Young Jewish boys have a special ceremony called *bar mitzvah* when they become full members of the Jewish community.

In very many ways their religion reminds Jewish people of their whole history, from 3000 years ago when God chose them as 'his people' to the present time.

The Christian World

JESUS CHRIST Christianity is the religion begun by Jesus Christ. Jesus lived in the country which is now called Israel and he was a Jew. His first followers were also Jews and Christianity grew up within the religion of the Jews — Judaism — and it is an offshoot of that religion. Later on, most Christians were non-Jews — Greeks, Romans and other neighbouring people — and Christianity became the religion of Europe.

Jesus lived almost 2000 years ago. In fact, our years — 1950, 1980, 1990 and all the rest — are counted from the year in which Christ was born. So 'A.D. 1950' means 'one thousand nine hundred and fifty years' *anno Domini* ('from the year of the Lord Jesus'). And '150 B.C.' means 'one hundred and fifty years before Christ'. Christmas is held on the date, December 25th, when Jesus Christ was born in a small village called Bethlehem.

Jesus lived for only thirty-three years and he was killed by the rulers of his country because he said that he was the 'Son of God'. Christians say that through Jesus God came into the world in a special way and gave a special message to people, not just through what Jesus said but also through how he lived.

Christians say that Jesus was a man — a Jew who lived and died at the age of thirty-three in Israel almost 2000 years ago — but that he was also God. Christians believe that God 'revealed' (manifested) himself in Jesus Christ.

Jesus said that God loves each one of us. God didn't need to create the world or any one of us. He could have got along quite happily without us. God created the world and everything in it, including us, out of pure love — out of the pure goodness of his heart. When you give someone a birthday present or a Christmas gift, you give it out of pure love — you don't have to give it. (If I have to give you something, then it's not a gift or a present). In the same way, the world and everything in it, including us, is God's present or gift.

Jesus also said that we must love other people in the same way as God loves us.

We must not harm other people
or treat them badly
or be cruel to them
or tell lies about them
or be envious of them
or kill them.

We must want only good things to happen to them: we must want them to be happy: we must wish them well. By living with people and suffering with them and even dying, Jesus tried to show how much God loved people. Jesus wasn't concerned at all about himself, or what would happen to him. He thought only of what would help other people. He was self-less.

If people followed his example and weren't selfishly concerned about themselves, Jesus said, they would be able to love God in the right way and also to love other people. If you love God, and if you love others, Jesus said, you will be able to live with God after you die.

Jesus formed a special group of twelve people who were called the 'Apostles' and he told them to carry on his work and to be like him. After his death all the followers of Jesus came together in a community which they called a 'Church'.

The Christian Church is first of all the community of those who follow Jesus' teaching and example: a church is also a building in which Christians meet and hold their special ceremonies.

In the Christian Church community there are a number of special people whose job it is to pass on the message of Jesus and help people to follow his example. They are called 'priests' or 'ministers'. The more important may become 'bishops', and 'archbishops', and in some of the Christian Churches there are also especially important people called 'popes' and 'patriarchs'.

After Jesus died his followers, particularly the Apostles, wanted to write down what they remembered of his sayings and of his life. These stories about Jesus were collected into four books which are called 'Gospels' (the good news brought by Jesus). Some of the Apostles also wrote letters ('epistles') to the early Christian groups and these letters were put together with the Gospels. This collection of writings is called the *New Testament* and Christians think that the teachings of the New Testament are very important in reminding them of Jesus' life.

Through the long history of the Christian religion there have been many holy men and women who followed Jesus' example very closely. They are called 'saints'. Jesus' mother, Mary, is the most important of the Christian saints. The

two main Apostles, Peter and Paul were also saints. In the Middle Ages in Europe (A.D. 1000 to A.D. 1400) there were saints such as Saint Francis of Assisi and Saint Catherine of Siena. Even in our own time holy men and women in the Christian Church have been called saints — for example, St. Bernadette of Lourdes, who was a young French girl and Saint Maximilian Kolbe, who was killed in a Nazi concentration camp during the last war.

Christians have special prayers and ceremonies for all the most important times in a person's life. When a Christian is a baby he or she is 'christened' or 'baptised' at a special ceremony, and when Christians get married they also have a special ceremony, and another when they are dying. Christians believe that through these ceremonies God helps people in a special way — to be good people, or to be good husbands and wives and parents, or to die happily.

The most important ceremony is the Eucharist which is held every Sunday in Christian Churches. In this ceremony Christians remember in a special way that Jesus loved them and gave them an example of how to love one another. In fact, they believe that at the ceremony of the Eucharist Jesus is once more among them.

Christianity is really a family of religions with many different children in the family. So there is a difference between the Christian Churches of Eastern Europe, such as the Greek Orthodox Church, the Russian Orthodox Church, the Ukranian Church, and the Christian Churches of Western Europe — the Roman Catholic Church, the Church of England, and the Protestant Churches which include the Lutheran, Presbyterian, Methodist, Uniting, and Baptist.

These Christian churches all say that they follow the example of Jesus Christ, but they differ about some of the teachings of Jesus and in the way they are organised. For example the Orthodox Churches have a patriarch as their leader, while the Roman Catholic Church has a pope, and the Church of England has the Archbishop of Canterbury as it's leader.

Many Christians think that it is a bad thing that there should be differences between the various Christian Churches and they hope that one day all these Churches may be able to join together in some way.

There are millions and millions of Christians. Most of them live in Europe, in the U.S.A. and Australia, and New Zealand and Africa.

Muhammad and Islam

Muhammad was an Arab. He was born about A.D. 570 in the city of Mecca which is in Saudi Arabia. Muhammad knew about the religion of Judaism and the Christian religion, but when he was forty years old he believed that God spoke directly to him and asked him to be his prophet or messenger.

ALLAH AND
THE PROPHET

God said to Muhammad:

You must make known to everyone that there is only one God and that His name is Allah. You must tell people to stop worshipping idols and many different gods and to obey only Allah.

Muhammad believed we owe all that we have — our life and everything else — to God. We therefore must give our complete devotion to God alone and we must not put anything else in the place of God. That is why Muhammad was so much against the worship of idols — the worship of things or people or spirits as though they were as important as God. That is also why he was against the worship of many gods (polytheism) since for him there could really be only one God (monotheism) who deserved our complete love and devotion.

ISLAM　The religion of Allah was called *Islam* (which means submitting to God and obeying Him) and the followers of Islam were called *Muslims*. Muslims believe that Islam is the most perfect religion there is; for them it is the best way of following God.

THE QUR'AN　God also told Muhammad how people must live if they are to be his true followers. Muhammad got someone to write down all that God had told him in a book that is called the *Qur'an* or *Koran*. Muslims believe that this book contains the very words of Allah himself and the *Qur'an* is very precious to them. Muslim children are taught to learn the *Qur'an* off by heart. ('Qur'an' means 'recitation' — the recitation of God's word.)

THE= PROPHET　Muslims believe that, although Muhammad was God's messenger or prophet, he was an ordinary man and not in any way a god. In the *Qur'an* it is said that the great Jewish leader, Moses, and also Jesus Christ, were God's prophets or messengers, but that Muhammad was God's last and most perfect messenger.

MUSLIMS' PRAYERS　When the Muslims are called to say their prayers the caller, or *muezzin*, sings: *God is most great. God is most great.*
　　　I tell you that there is no god except the One God.
　　　I tell you that Muhammad is the messenger of God.
　　　Come to prayer.

Muslims say prayers five times each day: at daybreak, at noon, in the middle of the afternoon, after sunset, and in the early part of the night.

They like to say their prayers together in a building called a *mosque* which is a kind of church. Everyone kneels on the ground behind the prayer-leader who is called the *imam* and all face in the direction of Mecca to show that they are united with all the other Muslims in the world.

THE PILLARS
OF THE FAITH As well as praying Muslims must do a number of other things:
- they must declare their faith by saying 'There is no god except the One God and Muhammad is the messenger of God';
- they must give money and help to poor people;
- they must fast for a whole month every year (the feast of *Ramadan*) by not eating or drinking during the day;
- they must try, at least once during their lives, to go on a pilgrimage to the Sacred Mosque in Mecca.

These five obligations are called the 'Pillars of the Faith'. In addition to these duties Muslims must not drink wine, they must not eat pork, they must not gamble. For Muslims there are in fact rules about almost everything — eating, drinking, dressing, bathing, table-manners, relationships between men and women, and so on. All these rules make up the sacred Law of Islam — called *Shari'a*.

The Muslims do not have priests, but they do have religious teachers who explain what the *Qur'an* means and guide the community of Muslims. Living in a community with other believers in Allah is very important for all Muslims. In fact you cannot be a true Muslim if you live by yourself. The community of all Muslims is called *Umma*.

Muhammad died in A.D. 632 and about two hundred years later there was a division among his followers and they broke into two separate groups. One group is called Sunni Muslims (this is the main body of Muslims) and the other group are called Shi'ite Muslims. The Sunni Muslims are mainly in Saudi Arabia, Egypt and the Arab States, and the Shi'ite Muslims are mainly in Iran, Iraq, Pakistan, East Africa and the Lebanon. One big difference between the two groups is that the Sunni Muslims see the *imams* just as prayer leaders, while the Shi'ite Muslims see their *imams* almost as prophets taking the place of Muhammad.

There is also a group of Muslims called *Sufis* who believe that they can come to know God directly and even to be one with God. The Sufis say that we must lose our own selves — we must not think of ourselves or worry about ourselves in any way — if we are to find God.

Muslims are spread all around the world — in Middle Eastern countries, Indonesia, Pakistan, Africa, Russia, and even in China. However, whatever their differences, all Muslims believe in *Islam* — that is, they believe in the One God, Allah, and they obey Allah's commands set out in the *Qur'an* by his prophet Muhammad and in the Islamic sacred Law or *Shari'a*.

Hinduism

GODS, YOGAS AND GURUS

Hinduism is not just one single religion but a collection of different forms of Indian religion. Hinduism began about 2000 years before the time of Jesus Christ but it did not have a founder, like Jesus Christ in the Christian religion or Muhammad in Islam. Neither did it have a sacred book like the Christian *New Testament* nor the Muslim *Qur'an*. Instead Hinduism has a large number of different writings which are believed to be of special religious importance.

The earliest Hindu teachings were contained in a series of religious writings called the *Vedas*. One part of the Vedas was called the *Upanishads* which are very important in Hinduism. Another important sacred writing of the Hindus was the *Bhagavad Gita* ('The Song of the Lord') which was written much later.

THE GODS For Hindus there is one main God, called *Brahman*. But this God shows itself in many different forms. These various forms of Brahman are also called gods, but they are really aspects or reflections or expressions of the one supreme God, Brahman. In fact, everyone and everything in the world is a reflection of Brahman.

The *Rig Veda*, one of the Hindu sacred writings, says: 'The Supreme Being (Brahman) is one, but the poets say that this Being is many'.

36

Some of the most important gods (aspects of reflections of Brahman) are: *Indra* the god of war, *Mitra* the sun god, *Varuna* the god who upholds the whole world, *Brahma* the creator god, *Vishnu* the god who preserves the whole world, *Shiva* the destroyer god.

These gods themselves also took various forms. So, one of the reflections or expressions of Vishnu is a god called Krishna, a favourite god of many Hindus. Krishna took a human form and there are many stories about him as a baby, as a young and playful boy, as a man who loved young women, and as a warrior. The *Bhagavad Gita* is mostly about Krishna: that is why it is called 'The Song of the Lord (Krishna)'.

GOD AND THE WORLD
For the Hindus the whole world, including the people in it, is a kind of reflection or expression or manifestation of Brahman. Some Hindus believe indeed that the whole world is part of God; people may think that the many things in the world are different and separate from God, but this, so they say, is an illusion (*maya*). In reality all these many different things are part of the one Brahman. We cannot really describe Brahman because it is much greater and more perfect that the many limited and imperfect forms through which it is expressed.

THE SELF: (ATMAN)
Apart from Brahman the most important thing for Hindus is the Self (*atman*). They believe that when you look deeply into yourself you discover your real Self, which lies behind the self which you show to other people. In fact some Hindus believe that this deep Self (*atman*) is the same as Brahman, so that if you know your true Self you know Brahman.

Hindus believe that you have lived before in another life and that when you die you are born again in another form — perhaps as another person, as an animal, as an insect.

If you lived a good life, you will be born again in a higher, more perfect form.

If you lived a bad life then you will be born again in a lower, less perfect, form.

If you are a very good and holy person you can finally escape the series of rebirths and come to be at one with Brahman. This is called 'liberation' (*moksha*).

All Hindus are born into one of four classes or 'castes': the Brahmin or priest class, the warrior class, the farmer and artisan class and the labouring class.

Each class or caste has its own special religious duties and rites and prayers which are called *dharma*. The *dharma* is the way of life you must follow if you are a member of a certain caste.

You can come to know and love God in various ways. These ways are called *yogas*.

One way of coming to know and love God is by doing good works without expecting any reward. This is called the *yoga of action (karma yoga)*.

Another way is to come to God through love of one of his reflections or expressions. Many Hindus, for example, love the God Krishna and pay devotion to him by saying prayers, and making offerings to images of him in temples. This is called the *yoga of love and devotion (bhakti yoga)*.

And there is a way of coming to God through wisdom and knowledge — meditating about God and concentrating your mind on him. This is called the *yoga of wisdom (jnana yoga)*.

To help you follows these 'ways' or yogas you need to have a teacher or *guru*. The guru gives you advice and tells you how to meditate and pray. He is not really a priest, but rather a religious teacher and adviser.

TEMPLES Although Hindus do not have a Church like Christians, they like to worship their gods in temples. The Hindu takes flowers and fruit or a gift to offer to his favourite god, and before he enters the temple he takes off his shoes to show his respect for the god. He then leaves his gift before a statue or image of the god and says some prayers to him. After he has finished he receives a blessing from holy men in the temple. Most Hindus also have little 'temples' in their homes and they light candles and burn incense before pictures of the gods.

Hindus spend a great deal of their time in saying prayers, meditating, visiting temples, and so on. Almost everything they do is bound up with their religion.

JISM TODAY Hindus have taken their religion with them wherever they have gone. Outside India there are Hindus in Fiji, Bali, Malaysia, Africa and many other countries. One of the most famous Hindus in our time was Mahatma Gandhi, who helped to bring about the independence of India in 1948. Gandhi preached a doctrine of 'non-violence', and said that we should never use force or violence against other people or engage in war against other countries. True Hindus, Gandhi said, must be lovers of peace.

41

The Buddha's Way of Enlightenment

In about 560 B.C. a man named Siddhartha was born in northern India in a village near the Himalayas. His family name was Gautama and his parents were rich. Siddhartha was brought up as a Hindu, but when he was twenty-nine years old he suddenly became aware that none of the things we love can last for very long.

So, people grow old, they get sick, they suffer, they die.

People who are strong may become weak.

Those who are beautiful may become ugly.

If we love someone then the one we love may leave us or die.

If we have lots of money we may very easily lose it all.

Because nothing lasts for very long, and because everything may
easily change, so Siddhartha thought, we can never really be happy
and content in this world,

no matter how many friends we may have

no matter how intelligent we may be

no matter how beautiful we may be

no matter how successful we may be

no matter how much money we may have.

I myself, even, can change in all kinds of ways so that I become
a very different person.

When Siddhartha became aware of all these things he was so upset that he left his wife and child and his own family, gave up all his possessions, and set out on a journey through Northern India in search of some Way of escaping from this life of suffering and unhappiness. But he was not able to find anyone who could help him, so he had to find the Way for himself.

THE BUDDHA'S
ENLIGHTENMENT

When he was thirty-five, after long searching, he finally discovered this Way and he became 'enlightened'. 'Buddha' means 'The enlightened one', and Siddhartha was called The Buddha (sometimes 'Gautama Buddha') from this time on. The Buddha wanted to teach other people about his Way, so he gathered a group of followers about him.

You must, the Buddha said to them, stop yourself from wanting or desiring things that give you pleasure.
You must not be concerned about yourself
You must train your mind to take no interest in the things of the world
You must be detached from all things in the world
You must even be detached from your own self.

When you are detached from the world and from your own self, the Buddha said, you can no longer be affected by the world and your self and made to suffer. When you are enlightened, the Buddha said, then you are free of all the things that attach or bind you to the world and which make you unhappy, and when you are truly free, or liberated, then you are truly happy, (though you do not want to be happy).

For the Buddha Enlightenment = Liberation = Happiness.

44

We cannot, however, say what this bliss or happiness is like, because it is so unlike anything else we know of. You have to experience it in order to know what it is like.

THE WHEEL OF REBIRTH Because he was brought up as a Hindu when he was young, the Buddha thought that when you died, your soul or spirit entered another body where it was 'reborn'. If you had lived a bad life you might be 'reborn' as a pig in your next life. If you had lived a good life you might become a better person in your next 'rebirth'. The Buddha was horrified by the thought of being 'reborn' time and time again, and he said that when you are truly 'enlightened' you will no longer be reborn: you will escape the 'wheel of rebirth'.

BUDDHIST LIFE To become 'enlightened' the Buddha said, you must live in a certain way
You must not hurt other people or animals
You must always tell the truth
You must also be honest
You must not steal
You must live as simply as you can.

The strictest followers of the Buddha live together in communities: they are called the *sangha*.
The Buddhist monks do not get married.
They give up all their belongings
They beg every day for their food
They study the teachings of the Buddha with a master
They meditate for hours each day and train their minds to be detached

They wear a simple orange robe.

The ordinary followers of the Buddha who remain in the world do as many of these things as they can.

FOLLOWING
THE BUDDHA The Buddha did not ever claim to be a God. He was simply an ordinary man who found a Way of escaping from the suffering and unhappiness of life and of achieving complete detachment and 'enlightenment'. Buddhists believe that if we follow this Way we too can become 'Buddhas' or 'enlightened ones'. It is no use saying prayers to God or expecting God to help you, the Buddha said. You may get help from a master, and you have the example of the Buddha's life and his teaching, but you must achieve 'enlightenment' for yourself.

The Buddha taught that there is no life, for those who are 'enlightened' and 'liberated', beyond this one. 'Enlightenment' takes place in this life and the 'enlightened' person will not be 'reborn'.

The Buddha died when he was eighty years of age and his teaching was carried on by his followers. After a time, his sayings were written down so that his followers could remember them and think about them.

DHIST GROUPS Although the Buddha's religion began in India, it gradually came to have very few Indian followers. But it became very popular in Sri Lanka and China, then in Tibet and Japan and Burma and Thailand. There are many different Buddhist groups and they understand the teachings of the Buddha in various different ways. However, all Buddhists follow the Way of the Buddha — The Way of Enlightenment and Liberation and Happiness.

Confucius and the Chinese Way

Confucianism is the ancient religion of China. From about 400 years before the time of Christ to A.D. 1900 the teachings of the wise man Confucius was the main religion of the Chinese people.

Confucius (Kung fu tzu was his Chinese name) was born in 551 B.C. Before that time the Chinese people had believed in following what they called the *Orders of Heaven*. They believed that over and above this world in which we live there is another world in which the spirits of the dead live. The King of that world is called 'The Lord Above' (*Shang-ti*) or 'Heaven' (*T'ien*). 'Heaven' gives orders which men must obey, or else 'Heaven' will punish them.

Confucius accepted many of these old ideas and added a lot of his own ideas to them. He said that if people followed his Way or *Tao* they would become good and holy and wise. They would become what he called 'noble minded people'.

Confucius thought that family life was very important. Children, he said, should respect and love their parents and parents should respect and love their children. In the same way in society people should respect their rulers and the rulers should care for their people.

Confucius said: *Children should respect their parents and people should respect their rulers, just as the world as a whole should respect the way of Heaven.*
And just as Heaven cares for the world, so rulers must care for their people, and parents must care for their children.

Confucius said that we must do five things if we wish to follow his Way.

- We must control our feelings so that we live in an orderly and harmonious way; and we must live in an orderly and harmonious way with other people.
  This is what Confucius called *Jen* or Goodness.
- We must try to live rightly, doing what we ought to do even though it might hurt us to do so. For example, we must not try to become wealthy or important by acting in a way that is not right.
  This is what Confucius called *I* or Justice.
- We must love and obey our parents and be considerate towards our brothers and sisters.
  This is what Confucius called *Hsia T'i* or Filial Respect.
- We must be loyal and considerate towards others. (One of Confucius' followers once asked him if there was one word that described what the most important thing in life was. Confucius replied, 'Perhaps the word "consideration" — do not do to others what you would not wish them to do to you.')
  This is what Confucius called *Shu* or Consideration.
- We must always be polite and courteous towards others and have good manners. This is what Confucius called *Li*, or Courtesy.

Confucius did not speak of God or whether we would go on living after our bodies die. He himself did not claim to be a god, nor even a prophet of God, nor did he set up a Church. Again, though he said we should respect the Way of Heaven he did not say that we should pray to the heavenly beings or try to know them directly. For Confucius it is what we do in this life, in our families and in society, that is important. The most perfect person is one who lives in harmony with himself and in harmony with other people. Such a person reflects the Way of Heaven in his life.

Confucius' teachings are collected in a book called the *Analects*. In that book Confucius had this to say:

You should behave well to your parents at home and to your elders outside the home.
You should be slow to make promises but quick to keep any promises you do make.
You should have kindly feelings towards everyone.
You should be a friend of everything that is good.
You should study the arts of writing, music, poetry, and archery.

If you live in this way, Confucius said, you will be a 'noble minded person'.

In the 1940s Mao Tse Tung and his Communist Party became the rulers of China and at first they said that Confucius' religion was old-fashioned and useless. (Communists think that religions are just fairy stories and that they stop people from making this world better.) But, despite this, Confucius' ideas have continued to influence Chinese people both in China itself and in Taiwan, Hong Kong, Singapore and other places where Chinese people live.

In Chinese, Confucius' name, 'Kung fu tzu', means 'The Wise Teacher Kung', and this is how, after more than 2,000 years, many Chinese people still think of him.

Australian Aboriginal Religion

THE SACRED LAND

The Australian Aboriginal people have been in Australia for almost 50,000 years, long before the Hindu religion began, long before the Buddha was born, long before Jesus Christ lived.

The Australian Aborigines live in small groups of about 100 people. There are the Aranda people, the Pintubi people, the Walbiri people, the Yolgnu people, the Dalabon people, the Pitjantjatjara people, and many, many other groups scattered north and south, east and west, all over the great continent of Australia.

Before white people came to Australia, there were more than 500 Aboriginal groups with more than 200 separate languages.

Most of these groups have their own particular form of religion. The Aranda people in Central Australia have their own religious stories and ceremonies; the Yolgnu people in Northern Australia have their own stories and ceremonies, and so do all the other groups.

THE GREAT SPIRITS All the Aboriginal religions belong to the same family. All Aborigines believe that at the beginning of everything (the 'Dreamtime' as white people call it) great Spirits came into the world, in the form of men and women and animals

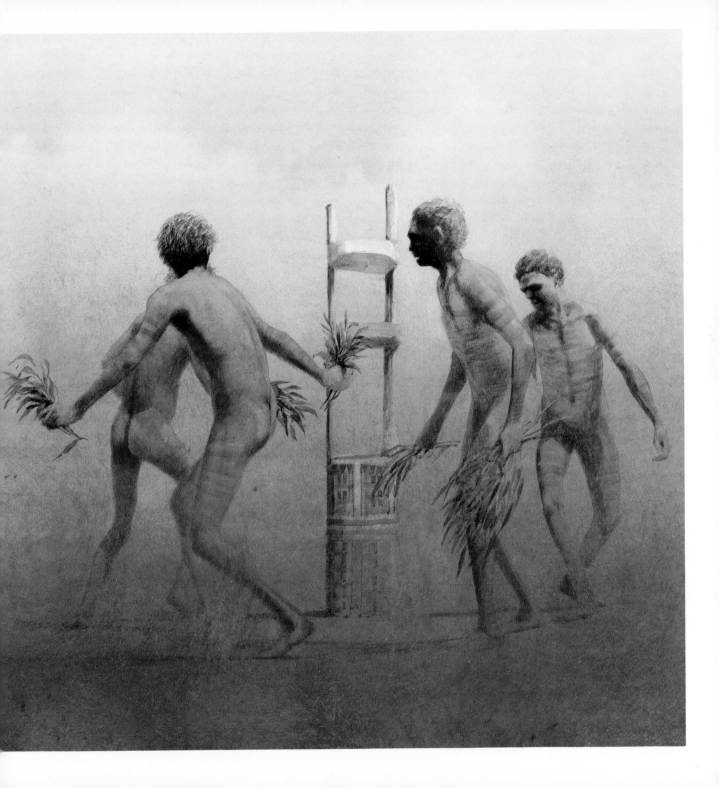

and birds, and made and shaped everything as it is now. When an Australian Aborigine looks at his people's land he believes that the rocks and hills and streams and waterholes were put there by the great Spirits who appeared on earth at the beginning of things.

'Those two rocks over there were thrown by the Spirit at one of his enemies', an Aborigine may say. *'That river was made by the Spirit Snake wriggling along the ground.'*

The great Spirits also left their power in special parts of the land and the Aborigines who live in such places can use that power to help themselves and to make sure that there are enough animals to hunt and plants and berries and nuts to eat. The Aborigines believe that they must care for these sacred places and not let other people use or destroy them.

The Aborigines think that each child has part of one of the great Spirits in him or her. So I might have part of the Wallaby Spirit in me and you might have part of the Emu Spirit in you. People have a special relationship with their Spirit and with all the other people who share in the life of that Spirit.

THE LAW The great Spirits who formed their land also gave the people who live on that land a 'Law' or way of living. Each group of Aborigines must follow the Law given to them by the Spirits. This Law tells them how to live together, what ceremonies to hold, what kind of people they can marry, and many other things.

The Law even tells them what parts of a kangaroo or other animals that different people in the group may eat.

In the past the Aborigines could not write, so they did not write down the

Law in sacred books. Instead the Law had to be remembered and passed down from father to son, and mother to daughter, in stories and songs about the Spirits.

CEREMONIES The Aborigines think that the time when young boys become men (about the age of 14), and when young girls become women, is very important. They have very special initiation ceremonies for this time. They also have special ceremonies for when people die.

The Australian Aborigines, in their traditional surroundings, live in a very simple way. They do not wear many clothes and they do not live in houses. They do not have weapons and tools made out of iron or other metals; they use axes and spears and tools made of wood and stone.

But, while they live very simply, their religion is very complex. Aborigines spend much more time on religious things — telling stories about the great Spirits, arranging ceremonies with music and songs and dances, looking after their sacred places — than on anything else.

THE SACRED LAND The great Spirits who gave each Aboriginal people its land and Law are not gods, like the Christian God or the Muslim Allah for example. What is most important for the Aboriginal people is their *land* which they believe was given to them by the Spirits. If an Aborigine cannot live on his people's land and hunt animals on it, and hold religious ceremonies on it, and care for the sacred places on it, and get in touch with the power left by the Spirits in it, then he cannot go on living.

For the Aborigine, the *land* of his people is like the Christian's God, or the

56

Muslim's Allah, because his whole life depends on his land. It is also like the Christian's Church, because it is through his land that the Aborigine can get in touch with the Spirits. When an Aborigine dies his own spirit goes back into the land where it came from and it rejoins the Spirit of which it was a part.

Compared with the millions of Christians and Hindus and Buddhists, the followers of Aboriginal religion are very, very few since there are now only about 150,000 Aborigines in Australia. But for most of them religion is the most important thing in their lives.

Religions of the North American Indians

Before white people came to North America there were more than 500 tribes of Red Indians. Most of them had come from Asia as long ago as 8000 B.C. These were some of the tribes: Sioux, Cree, Cherokee, Crow, Ohama, Seneca, Shoshoni, Cheyenne, Iroquois, Algonkin. These tribes usually lived separately from each other and often had their own language and their own religion.

THE SPIRIT WORLD Most of these religions claimed that there was a supernatural world over and above the world in which we live. Spirit beings dwell in that world. At the head of all the spirit beings there is a Supreme Being or Great Spirit. The Algonkin people called this Great Spirit *Manitou*.

They believed that the two worlds — the spirit world and our world — are in constant contact with each other. The spirits often enter into our world and some human beings are able to get in touch with the spirits.

THE WORLD TREE One of the stories of the North American Indians was about a 'world tree'. This tree has its roots in the earth but its branches reach into the world of the spirits. This story was told to make people aware that our world is connected with the world of the spirits. Some of the tribes had sacred poles which represent this world tree.

58

The Red Indians had many gods. The sun and the moon, the sky and the thunder were all thought to be gods. Some tribes believed that the earth was a goddess called 'Mother Earth'. The Huron tribe also thought that there was a vegetation goddess who made sure that corn and beans and pumpkins and other vegetables grew. This goddess, named Ataemtsic, tore up the world tree by its roots and made a hole in the sky. Her husband, who was the chieftain of heaven, was angry with her and threw her down through the hole to the earth. She then gave birth to twin sons, one good and one bad. The bad son killed Ataemtsic, but her good son formed the sun from her face and the moon and stars from her breasts, while out of her dead body there sprouted corn, beans and pumpkins. This story is meant to show that everything that grows and all our food come from the gods. The Huron people believed that the goddess Ataemtsic died for them so that they might have food and so live.

In many of the Red Indian tribes there were special people called 'medicine men' who were able to get in touch with the spirits. It was believed these medicine men could cure people from illness by getting the spirits to help them, and that they could make sure that the crops grew and that there was a good supply of animals to hunt.

The North American Indians held many religious ceremonies to praise the gods and ask for their help. In these ceremonies the medicine men played a central part; they led the prayers and the dances and acted as mediators between human beings and the spirits.

Sometimes these ceremonies took place around a sacred pole which

represented the link between the spirit world and the human world. The Red Indians believed that the spirits climbed down the pole and entered into the medicine men and then spoke through their mouths. The medicine man sometimes climbed to the top of the pole so as to speak to the spirits. All these beliefs and ceremonies emphasised how closely interwined the spirit world is with our human world.

For many of the North American Indians each person had a soul or spirit which can escape from his body when he is asleep and visit far off places. When his body dies his soul travels to the world of the dead, a world which is better and happier than this world. There will be plenty of buffalo to hunt and people will be able to feast and dance most of the time.

Some tribes thought that the Milky Way in the sky is the path taken by the souls of dead people on their way to the world of the dead. Bad people, they believed, cannot enter into that happy world. They either roam about as unhappy ghosts or are imprisoned in some place far away from heaven.

When white people came to North America most of the Red Indian tribes were destroyed and their religions were destroyed with them. Today very few of the tribes remain and fewer still live their traditional religious life. Many of those religions, which had lasted for over 10,000 years, no longer exist.

Reflections

We have seen some examples of the thousands of religions that have existed ever since human beings existed. Are all of these religions true? Or is one of them truer and better than the others? Or are all of them false?

Some people believe that all religions say the same things but in different forms. So, for example, the Hindu *Brahman* is the same as the Christian *God* and the Muslim *Allah*, though the Hindus describe Brahman and the Christians describe God and the Muslims describe Allah in different terms.

Other people say that the various religions are quite different from each other and that they express different aspects or facets of the Supreme Reality. So, for example, the Hindu *Brahman* expresses the fact that the many things in the world derive from the one Supreme Reality: the Christian *God* expresses the fact that the Supreme Reality is a person and that that person loves us; the Muslim *Allah* expresses the fact that the Supreme Reality is very much above us and different from everything else in the world. We need to combine all these different views in order to get a complete view of the Supreme Reality.

Some religious people — Hindus, Christians, Muslims and others — say that their own particular religion is the only true religion and that all the others are wrong.

Other religious people say that though their own religion is the true one, we can still learn a great deal from the other religions. So some Christians say that though Christianity is the truest and best religion, Christians can nevertheless learn from Buddhists, for example, that we must really lose ourselves in order to find God, or from Muslims that we depend on God for everything.

Some people say that all religions are fairy stories and that we have no need for religions at all. Such people are called atheists. According to them we can explain everything about the world and about ourselves without religion, but religious people, of course, say that you cannot explain the Big and Deep questions without believing in religion.

Whatever you think, there is no doubt that ever since human beings came to exist in this world they have had religions which helped them to understand the Big and Deep questions and so provided them with a map for living. For thousands and thousands of years Jews and Christians and Muslims and Hindus and Buddhists and Confucians and Australian Aborigines and American Indians have all lived in their religious worlds.